MA

American Moments

ABDO
Daughters

BROWN V. BOARD OF EDUCATION

By Alan Pierce

VISIT US AT
WWW.ABDOPUB.COM

Published by ABDO Publishing Company, 4940 Viking Drive, Suite 622, Edina, Minnesota 55435. Copyright © 2005 by Abdo Consulting Group, Inc. International copyrights reserved in all countries. No part of this book may be reproduced in any form without written permission from the publisher. ABDO & Daughters™ is a trademark and logo of ABDO Publishing Company.

Printed in the United States.

Edited by: Melanie A. Howard
Interior Production and Design: Terry Dunham Incorporated
Cover Design: Mighty Media
Photos: AP/Wide World; Corbis; John E. Phay collection, special collections, University of Mississippi Libraries; Library of Congress; South Caroliniana Library, University of South Carolina

Library of Congress Cataloging-in-Publication Data

Pierce, Alan, 1966-
    Brown v. Board of Education / Alan Pierce.
        p. cm. -- (American moments)
    ISBN 1-59197-725-8
    1. Brown, Oliver, 1918---Trials, litigation, etc.--Juvenile literature. 2. Topeka (Kans.). Board of Education--Trials, litigation, etc.--Juvenile literature. 3. Segregation in education--Law and legislation--United States--Juvenile literature. [1. African Americans--Civil rights.] I. Title: Brown versus Board of Education. II. Title III. Series.

KF228.B76P54 2005
344.73'0798--dc22
                                                        2004057449

CONTENTS

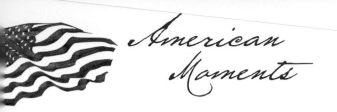
American Moments

A MOMENTOUS DECISION

On May 17, 1954, reporters rushed up the stairs to the courtroom of the U.S. Supreme Court. They had learned that momentous news was about to be announced. Chief Justice Earl Warren was prepared to read the court's decision in the case of *Brown v. Board of Education of Topeka*.

The result of this case was expected to have a major impact. For decades, many states separated black and white students into different schools. Separate schools were allowed for blacks and whites as long as the facilities were considered equal. This practice was known as "separate but equal." Now the Supreme Court had decided whether this practice, called segregation, was allowed by the Constitution.

As reporters filed into their seats, Justice Warren began to read the decision. Throughout much of the reading, no one knew which way the Supreme Court had ruled. Toward the end, the Court's position was clear. Warren said, "We conclude, unanimously, that in the field of public education the doctrine of 'separate but equal' has no place. Separate educational facilities are inherently unequal."

The word *unanimously* created a murmur of excitement in the courtroom. The justices had voted 9–0 to end segregation in public schools. Unanimous decisions were rare in highly controversial cases.

Outside the courtroom, the ruling caused more than a murmur. And unlike the Supreme Court, Americans were divided about the

Nettie Hunt explains the Brown v. Board of Education of Topeka *ruling to her daughter on the steps of the Supreme Court.*

decision. Many African Americans welcomed the ruling. Some felt as though the decision finally gave them a chance to succeed in the United States. But other African Americans were more guarded about the ruling. They had experienced a long history of unfair treatment, and they would wait to celebrate.

The reaction in the rest of the country was also split. Newspapers in the northern and western part of the country praised the ruling. In the South, some newspapers accepted the ruling, while others condemned it. Indeed, many leaders in the South promised to fight the decision. Virginia governor Thomas Stanley said, "I shall use every legal means at my command to continue segregated schools in Virginia."

These reactions indicated that *Brown v. Board of Education of Topeka* had not ended the fight over segregation in the schools. Rather, the battle was just beginning.

SEGREGATION

The Supreme Court's decision contended with a problem that had afflicted the United States for much of the country's history. Whites had long treated blacks as inferiors. Beginning in the seventeenth century, blacks from Africa were brought to the American colonies to work as slaves. They labored on tobacco, rice, and cotton plantations. As slaves, blacks were considered the property of their owners.

By the early nineteenth century, slavery became abolished in Northern states. However, this did not mean that blacks were welcomed into white society. Segregation existed in churches, restaurants, hotels, and other public places. It also prevailed in public schools. Schools for black students were almost always worse than schools for white students. Sometimes efforts were made to improve black schools. These attempts were often met with violence.

Most whites in the North felt superior to blacks. But this belief did not prevent many whites from hating slavery. Those who worked to end slavery were called abolitionists. Some abolitionists helped slaves escape to freedom. A system called the Underground Railroad helped thousands of slaves escape to the North and to Canada. Free blacks and Northern whites worked together to lead slaves out of the South.

The conflict over slavery helped lead to the Civil War between the Northern and Southern states. The Northern states were known as the

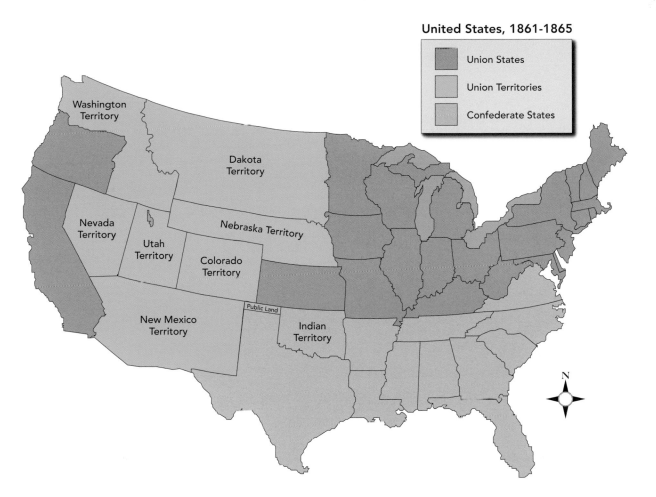

United States, 1861-1865

- Union States
- Union Territories
- Confederate States

Washington Territory

Dakota Territory

Nevada Territory

Idaho

Utah Territory

Nebraska Territory

Colorado Territory

New Mexico Territory

Public Land

Indian Territory

N

Union. In 1860 and 1861, eleven Southern states broke away from the United States. They formed the Confederate States of America. These states were all slave states. However, the slave states of Delaware, Maryland, Kentucky, and Missouri remained in the Union.

In 1865, the Civil War ended with a Union victory over the Confederacy. Northern leaders struggled with the question of how to admit the former Confederacy back into the United States. This process to restore these states to the Union was called Reconstruction.

The Union's triumph in the war had freed most of the slaves. But the well-being of the four million newly freed slaves posed a major challenge. The institution of slavery had not been officially abolished. In fact, slavery continued to exist in two slave states in the Union: Kentucky and Delaware. Some leaders in Congress believed that a constitutional amendment was needed to end slavery. Congress and most of the states approved the Thirteenth Amendment by December 1865. This amendment officially prohibited slavery.

Ratification of the Thirteenth Amendment failed to guard the rights of the newly freed slaves. Many Southern states passed laws called black codes. These codes were meant to limit the freedom of African Americans. For example, the codes contained vagrancy laws. These laws allowed unemployed African Americans to be arrested and fined. In some cases, African Americans were forced to work for farmers to pay off the money they owed.

The black codes convinced some members of Congress that African Americans needed more legal protection. Soon, the Radical Republicans worked on a constitutional amendment designed to protect the rights of African Americans. On July 28, 1868, the Fourteenth Amendment was ratified. This amendment guaranteed state and U.S. citizenship to African Americans.

The Fourteenth Amendment also accomplished another important aim. It guaranteed "the equal protection of the laws" to people in the states. This meant that similar people receive the same rights and must be treated similarly.

Congress also acted to protect the voting rights of African Americans in the South and throughout the country. During Reconstruction, laws had given Southern African Americans the right to vote. But some feared that Southern states would eventually deny this right to African Americans. In February 1869, Congress approved a constitutional amendment to guarantee African-American men the right to vote. It was ratified as the Fifteenth Amendment in March 1870.

CELEBRATION AT BALTIMORE ON MAY 19th 1870.

The Fifteenth Amendment was expected to improve the lives of African Americans.

Despite these constitutional amendments, African Americans continued to face segregation. But legal segregation was crumbling in the North. Massachusetts had outlawed segregation at inns. Also, African Americans could no longer be barred from public meetings in that state. In 1873, New York banned segregation in public accommodations.

In the South, segregation was becoming more widespread. By 1877, federal troops had withdrawn from the South, signaling the end of Reconstruction. Whites who had opposed Reconstruction then came to power in the Southern states. Subsequently, some states began to make segregation legal in the schools and on railroad passenger cars.

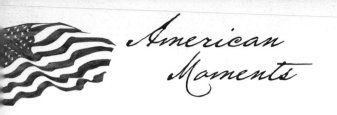

PLESSY

In 1890, the Louisiana legislature considered a law requiring separate railroad cars for black and white passengers. African-American members of the legislature fought the proposal. In addition, railroad companies objected to segregated cars. It was expensive to operate separate cars for black and white passengers. Despite this opposition, segregation on railroad cars became legal in Louisiana in July 1890.

African Americans continued to oppose the segregation of railroad cars. A group in New Orleans, Louisiana, formed the Citizens' Committee to Test the Constitutionality of the Separate Car Law. They worked with the East Louisiana Railroad to challenge segregation.

A man of African-American ancestry named Homer Plessy also participated in the plan. On June 7, 1892, Plessy bought a ticket to ride the East Louisiana Railroad from New Orleans to Covington, Louisiana. He attempted to board the whites-only car and was arrested for breaking the segregation law.

The case went before Judge John H. Ferguson in the Criminal District Court. Plessy's attorney, Albion Tourgée, argued that Louisiana's segregation law was unconstitutional. Ferguson disagreed and ruled against Plessy. In December 1892, the Louisiana Supreme Court supported Ferguson's decision. Plessy appealed to the U.S. Supreme Court to stop Ferguson from continuing the criminal case.

JIM CROW

In the South, laws that enforced segregation were known as Jim Crow laws. Jim Crow was the name of a musical routine that minstrel performer Thomas Dartmouth Rice first did in 1828. In the nineteenth century, minstrels were usually white performers who blackened their faces with makeup. As part of their performances, they portrayed African Americans in a biased and negative way.

It is unknown why Jim Crow became associated with segregation. However, by the 1840s, Jim Crow was used to describe segregated railroad cars in Massachusetts. Although forms of segregation existed in Northern states, Jim Crow laws were usually identified with Southern states.

Civil rights demonstrators protest Jim Crow.

In April 1896, the U.S. Supreme Court heard the arguments in the case of *Plessy v. Ferguson.* On May 18, the Court upheld Louisiana's law to segregate railroad cars. This decision was based on the "separate but equal" doctrine. This idea maintained that segregated facilities were legal as long as they were equal.

Chief Justice Henry Billings Brown issued the Court's majority opinion. In the opinion, Brown asserted that segregation did not place a "badge of inferiority" on African Americans. Brown wrote, "If this be so, it is not by reason of anything found in the act, but solely because the colored race chooses to put that construction upon it."

Plessy v. Ferguson dealt with the segregation of railroad cars. But Brown also cited laws that set up segregation in other areas. Brown wrote, "The most common instance of this is connected with the establishment of separate schools for white and colored children . . . "

Justice John Marshall Harlan was the only member of the Supreme Court to disagree with the ruling. He wrote his own opinion. Harlan wrote, "Our Constitution is color-blind, and neither knows nor tolerates classes among citizens. In respect of civil rights, all citizens are equal before the law."

Harlan also understood the significance of the Court's decision. He wrote that if a state had the power to segregate passenger cars, then the state could force blacks and whites to use different sides of the streets. Harlan proved to be right. In the next several years, legal segregation expanded beyond railroad cars. Southern states established segregation in parks, hospitals, theaters, and the workplace. Signs that read Whites Only and Colored Only marked facilities throughout the South.

Henry Billings Brown

NAACP

The Supreme Court's decision in *Plessy v. Ferguson* marked a serious setback for the rights of African Americans. However, the ruling failed to end the struggle for civil rights. In 1909, several African Americans and whites met in New York City, New York, to form an organization. This group was dedicated to promoting equality for African Americans. The next year, the organization adopted the name National Association for the Advancement of Colored People (NAACP).

During the next several years, the NAACP waged legal battles against discrimination. The organization relied on lawyers to volunteer their services. Nevertheless, the NAACP won important victories. In 1917, the U.S. Supreme Court ruled that laws preventing African Americans from moving into white neighborhoods were unconstitutional. Lawyer and NAACP president Moorfield Storey had argued the case before the Supreme Court.

By 1930, the NAACP prepared to pursue a wider fight against segregation. As part of this plan, the association hired New York attorney Nathan Ross Margold to write a study. Margold issued a report in 1931. His report recommended a legal attack against state segregation laws. The report also encouraged the NAACP to focus on the inequality between black and white public schools. Margold believed this strategy would force states to improve black schools or give up on segregation.

In 1935, the NAACP established its legal department to carry out Margold's recommendations. The NAACP selected Charles H. Houston to lead the association's legal efforts. Houston was an African-American attorney with a distinguished legal career. He was also dean of Howard University School of Law in Washington DC.

The Margold Report recommended challenging segregation in public schools. But Houston favored a strategy that first fought segregation in graduate and professional schools. Almost no graduate or professional schools existed for African Americans in the South. By not having these schools, many states were not complying with the doctrine of "separate but equal." Houston believed that a successful fight against segregation at these schools would eventually lead to desegregation of the high schools and elementary schools.

Charles H. Houston

15

Meanwhile, one of Houston's former students approached him about a case. The former student's name was Thurgood Marshall, and he was an attorney in Baltimore, Maryland. Marshall had accepted the case of an African-American man named Donald Murray. In 1934, Murray had applied to enter the University of Maryland Law School. However, the school rejected Murray because of his race. Houston agreed to help Marshall with the case.

Murray sued the University of Maryland Law School to be considered for admission. The lawsuit became known as *Murray v. Maryland*. In June 1935, Houston and Marshall argued the case in Baltimore City Court. Judge Eugene O'Dunne presided over the trial. Marshall attacked the "equal" part of the "separate but equal" doctrine established by *Plessy v. Ferguson*. The state of Maryland did not have equal facilities for Murray, Marshall argued. This was evident by the fact that Maryland had no law school for African Americans.

On June 25, Judge O'Dunne announced his decision. He ordered the university's president, Raymond Pearson, to admit Murray to the law school. The university appealed. But in January 1936, the Maryland Court of Appeals agreed with O'Dunne's decision. Murray was allowed to enter the law school, and he later graduated.

Murray's admission to the University of Maryland Law School marked an important moment. It was not the first victory against segregation. But it was one of the first triumphs against segregation in education.

Opposite page: *Thurgood Marshall (left), Donald Murray (center), and Charles Houston prepare for trial.*

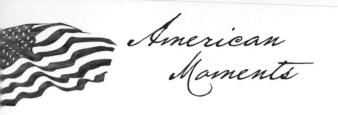

LEGAL VICTORIES

The NAACP legal department underwent a change after *Murray v. Maryland*. In 1938, Houston resigned from his position as head of the NAACP legal department. At the age of 30, Marshall took over the legal duties at the NAACP.

In 1940, the NAACP formed a new organization to carry out the legal fight for equal rights. This organization was called the NAACP Legal Defense and Educational Fund Inc. (LDF). The NAACP created this organization so that the legal fund would receive tax benefits. Marshall led the LDF.

Marshall and the LDF continued the legal campaign against segregation throughout the 1940s. Marshall agreed to represent an African-American man named Heman Sweatt. In February 1946, Sweatt applied to the University of Texas Law School in Austin. The university rejected Sweatt's application because he was African American. Sweatt then sued Theophilus Painter, the president of the University of Texas, to be considered for admission.

In June, a district court judge gave the state of Texas two choices. The state could admit Sweatt to the all-white law school or establish a law school for African Americans. Eventually, the state created an African-American law school in Austin. The school had a staff of three people, and it was located in three basement rooms of an office building.

LDF lawyers (from left to right): *Louis Redding, Robert L. Carter, Oliver W. Hill, Thurgood Marshall, and Spottswood W. Robinson III*

By April 1950, the case of *Sweatt v. Painter* went to the U.S. Supreme Court. Marshall did not simply argue that the facilities of black and white law schools were unequal. He also asserted that segregation hurt African-American law students. Segregation separated African-American law students from students they would expect to work with later. Moreover, segregation prevented African-American students from sharing ideas and attitudes with another group of students.

On June 5, Chief Justice Frederick M. Vinson issued the Court's opinion. He said the two law schools were unequal. Also, Sweatt had a constitutional right to an education that was equivalent to what other races received. Finally, Vinson stated that the equal protection

19

guarantee of the Fourteenth Amendment required the University of Texas Law School to admit Sweatt. The Supreme Court decision was historic. For the first time, the Court had ordered a state to admit an African-American student into an all-white school.

Another segregation case was decided at the Supreme Court the same day. This case was called *McLaurin v. Oklahoma State Regents for Higher Education*. In 1948, an African-American teacher named George W. McLaurin wished to earn a doctorate degree in education. He applied to the University of Oklahoma, but was denied admission.

Later that year, a panel of three judges ruled that the state was obligated to provide McLaurin with the education he wanted. The University of Oklahoma admitted McLaurin. But the university managed to segregate McLaurin. He could not sit in the classroom with white students. Instead, he had to sit in a room outside of class. McLaurin was also isolated from white students in the library and cafeteria. The university finally allowed McLaurin into the classroom where a railing surrounded his seat. The railing displayed a sign that read Reserved for Colored. Other students took down the railing.

McLaurin continued to use the courts to protest his treatment. In April 1950, LDF attorney Robert L. Carter argued the case of *McLaurin v. Oklahoma State Regents for Higher Education* before the U.S. Supreme Court.

The Supreme Court ruled in McLaurin's favor. The opinion said the restrictions placed on McLaurin hindered his ability to learn. In addition, the Court ruled that the Fourteenth Amendment prohibited states from treating people differently because of race. McLaurin must receive the same treatment as other students, the Court decided.

George W. McLaurin is forced to sit apart from white students at the University of Oklahoma.

    The decisions in the *McLaurin* and *Sweatt* cases were important triumphs. But they did not achieve total victories against segregation. The Supreme Court had not rejected the "separate but equal" doctrine of *Plessy v. Ferguson*. And segregation remained firmly established in the elementary and high schools of all or part of 21 states.

TOPEKA

High schools and elementary schools for black and white students were separate, but they were hardly equal. All-black schools were worse off than white schools. Conditions were especially bad in the South. School buildings for African-American students were often in terrible shape. African-American students also received the broken or used furniture from white schools.

One county in Mississippi provides an example of the poor educational conditions for African Americans. In Sunflower County, no high school existed for African Americans. And in the county's African-American elementary schools, many of the teachers had only a fourth-grade education.

School boards in the South also spent less money on African-American students than on white students. For example, records show that in 1949 and 1950, Mississippi spent $119.09 per white student. In contrast, $27.45 was spent per black pupil. At the same time, Georgia spent $131.67 per white student and $70.99 per black student.

By 1948, the fight against segregation was being fought in Topeka, Kansas. Segregation was not as prevalent in Topeka as it was in the South. For example, the waiting areas at the city's bus and train stations were not segregated. Also, the city's high school was mostly integrated. However, the high school's sports teams were separated by race. Moreover, the city's elementary schools were

*The Williams School, an African-American school
in Sunflower County, Mississippi, in 1949*

completely segregated. The city had 18 schools for white students
and 4 schools for black students.

McKinley Burnett wanted to end segregation in the elementary
schools. He was the president of the Topeka chapter of the NAACP.
In the fall of 1948, he presented petitions to the Topeka Board of
Education, asking that segregation be stopped. For two years, the
board ignored these requests. Finally, in August 1950, the NAACP

in Topeka contacted the association's leadership in New York City. Burnett was ready to file a lawsuit to end segregation in the elementary schools.

In order to have a lawsuit, the NAACP needed parents to sue the school board. One of those who agreed to take part in the lawsuit was Oliver Brown. He was a 32-year-old welder for the railroad. Brown also served as an assistant pastor for a Methodist church.

Brown's 7-year-old daughter, Linda, lived 7 blocks from the all-white Sumner School. But segregation prevented her from attending Sumner. Instead, she went to the all-black Monroe School, which was 21 blocks from her home. Not only was the trip to Monroe longer, it was also riskier. Linda had to cross a dangerous railroad switchyard to catch her bus ride to school.

Linda Brown went with her father when he tried to enroll her into the all-white Sumner School near her home. She was denied admission.

On February 28, 1951, the NAACP filed the lawsuit in the U.S. District Court for Kansas. Oliver Brown was one of 13 parents who had joined the lawsuit to oppose segregation. Because he was listed as the first parent, the case was called *Brown v. Board of Education of Topeka*. Trial was set for June 25 in a Topeka courtroom.

At the trial, attorney Robert L. Carter led the parents' and LDF's case against segregation. Carter focused on the harmful effects that segregation had on African-American students. Several experts in psychology and education testified about these effects. They said that segregation made African-American students feel inferior. This feeling of inferiority hurt their motivation to learn.

In August, Judge Walter Huxman issued the court's opinion. Huxman refused to halt segregation of Topeka's elementary schools. He noted that the Supreme Court had not rejected the doctrine of "separate but equal." However, Huxman indicated that he believed that segregation hurt African-American students. Part of the opinion said, "Segregation of white and colored children in public schools has a detrimental effect upon the colored children. The impact is greater when it has the sanction of the law; for the policy of separating the races is usually interpreted as denoting the inferiority of the Negro group."

Judge Huxman's opinion was not the final decision in *Brown v. Board of Education of Topeka*. The case would eventually go before the U.S. Supreme Court. Also, *Brown* was not the only case to challenge segregation. Other parents and children were in the courts fighting segregation.

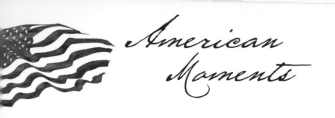

ASSAILING SEGREGATION

Parents and NAACP members did not always take the lead to oppose segregation in the schools. In Virginia, students led the fight for desegregation. Barbara Johns was a 16-year-old student at Robert R. Moton High School in Prince Edward County. She was a member of the student council and chorus. These activities allowed her to travel outside her hometown of Farmville and to compare her school to others. She realized that her school was in terrible condition.

Johns and other members of the student council decided to take action. They planned a strike and demanded the promise of a better high school building. On April 23, 1951, Johns led 450 Moton students on a strike. A local minister helped the students contact the NAACP. Soon, LDF lawyers were involved on behalf of the students.

A month after the strike, the NAACP filed a lawsuit for 117 Moton students. These students now wanted something more than a new high school. In the lawsuit, they asked the state of Virginia to abolish segregation in the schools. The lawsuit was called *Davis v. County School Board of Prince Edward County*. Davis was the name of Dorothy E. Davis. Her name appeared first on the list of students suing the school board.

The trial for the case started on February 25, 1952. It lasted five days. A week later, the three federal judges issued their decision.

The auditorium of Robert R. Moton High School

The judges ordered the Prince Edward School Board to improve facilities for African-American students. But the judges refused to renounce segregation. In fact, they defended it as a longtime custom in Virginia.

Kansas and Virginia were not the only places where African Americans resisted discrimination in the public schools. In South Carolina, the Reverend Joseph Albert DeLaine was a schoolteacher. He saw the discrimination that African-American students faced in Clarendon County. For example, school buses were available for white students but not for blacks. In the 1940s, he encouraged parents to resist this unfair treatment against their children. In 1949, DeLaine had more success when he brought in the LDF.

That year, several parents and Marshall filed a lawsuit against the school district. The lawsuit was titled *Briggs v. Elliott*. Harry Briggs was one of the parents suing the school district. Roderick Elliott was the name of the chairman of the local school district.

The lawsuit emphasized the unequal conditions that African-American students experienced in Clarendon. Schools for whites were made out of bricks and stucco. Black students attended schools that were little more than shacks. During that school year, the school district spent $149 per white student but only $43 per black student. At first, the lawsuit requested better school facilities for African-American students. Later, *Briggs v. Elliott* aimed to end segregation in the schools.

Trial began on May 28, 1951. A panel of three judges heard the case in Charleston, South Carolina. In June, the judges issued their ruling. They ordered the school district to provide equal educational facilities for African-American students. However, two of the judges denied the request to abolish segregation. Judge J. Waties Waring disagreed. He criticized segregation in a separate opinion. Waring wrote that "segregation in education can never produce equality and that it is an evil that must be eradicated."

African Americans also challenged segregation in the District of Columbia. An African-American barber named Gardner Bishop had organized a student boycott of an Africa-American junior high school. Bishop was upset that the school was overcrowded while white schools had plenty of space for students.

In order to make progress in his struggle, Bishop joined forces with the NAACP. He became enthusiastic when he learned that LDF attorney James Madison Nabrit Jr. intended to tackle segregation. On September 11, 1950, Bishop took 11 African-American students to the new white John Philip Sousa Junior High School in Washington DC. Bishop tried to enroll the students, but he was denied. In early 1951, Nabrit filed a lawsuit in U.S. District Court. The case was called *Bolling v. Sharpe*. Spottswood Thomas Bolling Jr. was one of the students who had accompanied Bishop to the white school. C. Melvin Sharpe was the president of the Board of Education of the District of Columbia.

Nabrit did not argue that black schools were inferior to white schools in the District of Columbia. Instead, he argued against

The DeLaine family's home in Summerton, South Carolina, was burned in response to Joseph Albert DeLaine's work for desegregation.

segregation. He said the District of Columbia needed to offer a reason for denying African-American students enrollment in white schools.

The school board maintained that *Bolling v. Sharpe* should be dismissed. After all, the courts had recently found the District of Columbia's system of segregation in the schools to be legal. In April 1951, U.S. District Court judge Walter M. Bastain agreed with the school board. Nabrit then prepared the case for the U.S. Court of Appeals.

Two other cases happened in Delaware in 1951. But they involved the same issue. African-American parents sued to integrate the schools. In one case, parents were outraged about the condition of Howard High School in Wilmington, Delaware. This case was titled *Belton v. Gebhart*. Ethel Belton was one of eight African-American parents who filed the lawsuit. Gebhart was the name of Francis B. Gebhart, who served on the state board of education.

In the other case, an African-American parent named Sarah Bulah filed the lawsuit of *Bulah v. Gebhart*. She filed the lawsuit because school buses in her area transported white students but not black students. Bulah had to drive her daughter to school in Hockessin, Delaware. These cases were eventually heard by Chancellor Collins J. Seitz in the Court of Chancery.

In April 1952, Seitz issued his opinion. He wrote that the black students in the lawsuit were entitled to attend white schools. This was the first time a state court had ordered an all-white public school to admit African-American children. However, Seitz did not rule that segregation was illegal. He believed that was a decision for the U.S. Supreme Court to make.

DID YOU KNOW?

Did you know that President Harry S. Truman ordered the desegregation of the U.S. armed forces?

Tensions surrounding segregation in the military reached a breaking point in the 1940s. Murders of African-American veterans had inflamed the already heated argument over whether or not to integrate the military.

African-American leader A. Philip Randolph urged President Truman to desegregate the armed forces. On June 29, 1948, he told President Truman that African Americans were planning to resist the draft if the president did not desegregate the military.

Truman, who had already been advised to desegregate the military, issued Executive Order 9981 on July 26, 1948. The order called for the desegregation of the military. On May 11, 1949, the Air Force became the first branch to have its desegregation proposal approved. The Navy soon followed on June 7.

A desegregated military unit in Korea in the 1950s

Desegregating the Army proved difficult. But in January 1950, the Army's proposal for desegregating its units was finally approved. Integration did not happen, however, until the Korean War. During the war, troop shortages caused the Army to abandon segregation. In October 1953, the Army announced that 95 percent of its African-American soldiers were serving in integrated units. The desegregation of the military had become one of the first victories in the battle to end segregation.

JUSTICE WARREN'S DECISIONS

The five lawsuits had failed to topple the "separate but equal" doctrine. Eventually, these cases were appealed to the U.S. Supreme Court. In early June 1952, the U.S. Supreme Court added *Brown v. Board of Education* to its court schedule. In addition, the Supreme Court included the other cases with the *Brown* case.

In the Supreme Court, Marshall and other LDF lawyers would face an imposing attorney. John W. Davis represented South Carolina in the *Briggs v. Elliott* case. He also led the overall side that supported segregation. Davis had an impressive legal and political career. He had been involved in dozens of Supreme Court cases. Davis had also served as a congressman and had been a candidate for president.

Marshall and Davis would argue before the nine Supreme Court justices. In addition to Chief Justice Vinson, they were Hugo L. Black, Harold H. Burton, William O. Douglas, Tom C. Clark, Felix Frankfurter, Robert H. Jackson, Sherman Minton, and Stanley F. Reed.

John W. Davis

U.S. Supreme Court justices pose for their portrait in 1950. In front from left to right are Felix Frankfurter, Tom C. Clark, Hugo L. Black, Robert H. Jackson, Frederick M. Vinson. In back are Harold H. Burton Stanley F. Reed, Sherman Minton, and William O. Douglas.

The hearing began on December 9. Much of the argument repeated points that had been made in the district courts. Marshall and the other NAACP lawyers argued against the *Plessy* decision. They said that segregation discriminated against African Americans. This discrimination violated the Fourteenth Amendment, which guaranteed equal protection under the law.

Davis challenged the NAACP lawyers about the Fourteenth Amendment. He argued that Congress passed the Fourteenth Amendment and then soon set up segregation in the District of

Columbia's schools. Therefore, school segregation was not in conflict with the Fourteenth Amendment.

After the hearing, the Supreme Court did not make a decision. Instead, the Court scheduled another hearing about the Fourteenth Amendment. The justices wanted to know more about the historical circumstances surrounding the passage of the Fourteenth Amendment in 1868. They also wanted to find out more about Congress's intentions behind the Fourteenth Amendment. This hearing was scheduled in December 1953.

Before the second hearing was held, the Supreme Court underwent an important change. Chief Justice Vinson died on September 8, 1953. President Dwight D. Eisenhower nominated California governor Earl Warren to replace Vinson. In October, Warren was sworn in as chief justice on the Court.

On December 7, 1953, lawyers for both sides of the segregation cases argued about the Fourteenth Amendment. However, neither side provided a clear answer about Congress's position on school segregation in 1868.

After these hearings, Warren told the other judges that he thought that segregation could no longer be defended. "I don't see how in this day and age we can set any group apart from the rest and say that they are not entitled to exactly the same treatment as all others," Warren said.

However, Warren wanted a unanimous decision if the Court ended school segregation. A unanimous decision would send a strong message that segregation was wrong. On the other hand, a split vote would send a weak message to the American public.

Opposite page: *Chief Justice of the Supreme Court Earl Warren*

Warren worked hard with the other justices to obtain a unanimous vote against school segregation. He also began to write a legal opinion that all the justices could accept. Warren wrote two opinions. One was for *Brown v. Board of Education*. The other was for the *Bolling v. Sharpe* case. Two opinions were necessary because *Bolling v. Sharpe* dealt with segregation in the District of Columbia, while the other cases involved states. The Fourteenth Amendment only applied to cases in the states.

On May 17, 1954, Warren read the two opinions at the courthouse of the U.S. Supreme Court. He read the opinion for *Brown v. Board of Education* first. "We come then to the question presented: Does segregation of children in public schools solely on the basis of race, even though the physical facilities and other 'tangible' factors may be equal, deprive the children of the minority group of equal educational opportunities? We believe that it does."

With these statements, Warren announced that school segregation was unconstitutional. Warren went on to say that school segregation violated the Fourteenth Amendment because African-American students were denied equal protection under the law.

Warren also read the decision in the *Bolling v. Sharpe* case. School segregation in the District of Columbia was found to be unconstitutional because it violated the Fifth Amendment. The Fifth Amendment guarantees the right to liberty. Segregation denied the right to liberty to African-American students in the District of Columbia, the Court ruled.

MR. CIVIL RIGHTS

Brown v. Board of Education of Topeka was one of many cases that Thurgood Marshall argued before the U.S. Supreme Court. In his career at the NAACP Legal Defense and Educational Fund Inc., Marshall and his aids argued 32 cases before the Court. They won 29 of these cases. Marshall's work as an attorney helped him earn the nickname "Mr. Civil Rights."

In 1961, President John F. Kennedy appointed Marshall to serve as a judge for the U.S. Court of Appeals for the Second Circuit. Some Southern senators opposed Marshall's nomination, and he did not begin to serve as a judge until 1962.

Thurgood Marshall

Three years later, President Lyndon B. Johnson made Marshall solicitor general. This meant that Marshall represented the U.S. government before the Court. As solicitor general, Marshall helped bring about Miranda warnings. These warnings require police officers to inform suspects of their rights.

In 1967, Johnson appointed Marshall to the U.S. Supreme Court. This made him the first African American ever to be a Court justice. While serving on the Court, Marshall supported civil rights and opposed discrimination. Although he hoped to serve longer, poor health forced Marshall to leave the Court in 1991. He died in 1993 at the age of 84. To this day, he is known as one of America's greatest civil rights defenders.

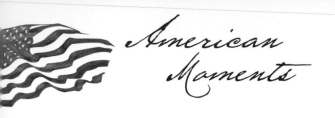

"ALL DELIBERATE SPEED"

A year later, the Supreme Court held hearings about how to implement school desegregation. These hearings are often referred to as *Brown II*. The Supreme Court had a difficult time deciding how to implement desegregation. In some ways, this step was more challenging than the decision to rule against *Plessy*. The justices were very concerned about the reaction toward school desegregation, especially in the South. Justice Black, who was from Alabama, warned that some school districts might close their schools rather than end segregation.

The Court needed to decide whether desegregation should be implemented immediately or gradually. Worries about violent white reaction to desegregation played a role in the Court's decision. Eventually, the Court decided that desegregation should occur gradually.

The Supreme Court ordered that schools should be integrated with "all deliberate speed." However, the phrase "all deliberate speed" was left open to interpretation. Speed implied that desegregation should happen quickly. But deliberate means slow and steady. In many cases, integration happened slowly in some places in the South.

The Supreme Court justices had been right to be concerned about an angry reaction. Many Southern leaders protested against desegregation. U.S. senators Strom Thurmond of South Carolina and

Senator Strom Thurmond testifies against civil rights legislation in 1957.

Harry Byrd of Virginia produced the Southern Manifesto. In March 1956, more than 90 members of Congress signed this statement. One part of the manifesto said, "We pledge ourselves to use all lawful means to bring about a reversal of this decision which is contrary to the Constitution and to prevent the use of force in its implementation."

Virginia took one of the strongest stands against integration. In 1956, the state adopted a strategy that was known as Massive Resistance. This plan called for closing public schools that were ordered to desegregate. However, the state also provided money for white students to attend private schools. Under this plan, the state closed some schools in Norfolk, Charlottesville, and Warren County. By 1959, a federal court had prohibited Massive Resistance and desegregation was attempted in some Virginia schools.

More than a year later, Little Rock, Arkansas, became a battleground over school integration. The city school board had approved a desegregation plan. According to this plan, nine African-American students would attend classes at Central High School in the fall of 1957. However, Arkansas governor Orval Faubus opposed this action. He ordered national guardsmen to block the African-American students from entering the school.

President Eisenhower was forced to act. Faubus was violating the Supreme Court. Eisenhower ordered federal troops to escort the nine students to school. Under federal pressure, the school became desegregated.

In the 1960s, school districts began using busing to bring about integration. This meant that students in public schools were transported by buses outside their neighborhoods to attend school. Many whites opposed busing. But in 1971, the Supreme Court made a decision about busing to achieve desegregation. In the case of *Swann v. Charlotte-Mecklenburg Board of Education*, the Court ruled that busing was an acceptable practice.

The struggle to desegregate schools is ongoing. But *Brown v. Board of Education* has given rise to triumphs as well as to frustrations. The Supreme Court decision has provided African Americans with educational opportunities they never had before 1954. These opportunities have made it possible for African Americans to get better jobs and to lead better lives. And just as importantly, *Brown v. Board of Education* permitted the United States to be a better country. On May 17, 1954, the Supreme Court challenged the country to live up to its ideals of justice and equality.

Opposite page: George E.C. Hayes, Thurgood Marshall, and James Madison Nabrit Jr. congratulate each other after winning the Brown *case.*

TIMELINE

1865   On December 6, the Thirteenth Amendment is ratified.

1868   On July 28, the Fourteenth Amendment is ratified.

1870   On February 3, the Fifteenth Amendment is ratified.

1896   On May 18, the U.S. Supreme Court issues its decision on *Plessy v. Ferguson*. This establishes the "separate but equal" doctrine.

1910   The National Association for the Advancement of Colored People (NAACP) adopts the organization's name.

1935   The NAACP establishes its legal department.

1936   Maryland Court of Appeals upholds *Murray v. Maryland* decision.

1940   The NAACP sets up the Legal Defense and Educational Fund Inc.

1950   U.S. Supreme Court upholds *Sweatt v. Painter* decision, orders a state to admit an African-American student to a white school for the first time.

       U.S. Supreme Court upholds *McLaurin v. Oklahoma State Regents for Higher Education* decision.

1951   On February 28, the NAACP files the *Brown v. Board of Education of Topeka* lawsuit in U.S. District Court.

       In April, Judge Walter M. Bastain dismisses Washington DC segregation case *Bolling v. Sharpe*.

In *Briggs v. Elliott*, judges order Clarendon County, South Carolina, to improve African-American schools. However, two of the three vote not to strike down segregation.

In August, the U.S. District Court refuses to stop segregation in Topeka, citing *Plessy v. Ferguson*.

1952

Federal judges order Prince Edward County in Virginia to improve African-American schools in *Davis v. County School Board of Prince Edward County* in March. However, they uphold segregation.

In April, Chancellor Collins J. Seitz rules on *Belton v. Gebhart* and *Bulah v. Gebhart* in Delaware. White public schools are ordered to admit black students for the first time.

On December 9, the U.S. Supreme Court hears *Brown v. Board of Education* for the first time. The Supreme Court schedules another hearing for the following December.

1953 The U.S. Supreme Court hears *Brown* again on December 7.

1954 On May 17, the U.S. Supreme Court issues the *Brown* decision. The "separate but equal" doctrine is overturned; Court overturns decision in *Bolling v. Sharpe*.

1955 In *Brown II*, the U.S. Supreme Court decides that schools throughout the nation should desegregate with "all deliberate speed."

1957 Nine African-American students in Little Rock, Arkansas, challenge segregation in Central High School in the fall.

American Moments

FAST FACTS

As early as 1787, blacks were committed to making education accessible for their children. In that year, blacks petitioned the Massachusetts legislature to admit black children to Boston's public schools. Boston's public schools were finally integrated in 1855.

Brown v. Board of Education of Topeka was not the first time that segregation had been challenged in Topeka's schools. In 1903, an African-American man named William Reynolds tried to enroll his son in a school for whites. He sued the school board, but the Kansas Supreme Court upheld the school's segregation policy.

In 1980, the University of Maryland Law School named its new library after Thurgood Marshall. The honor took place 44 years after Marshall won a lawsuit against the school to admit African-American student Donald Murray.

Monroe School was closed in 1975 because of falling enrollment. The building was used as a warehouse and as a meeting place. Since 1992, Monroe School has been part of the *Brown v. Board of Education* National Historic Site. The site preserves the history of the *Brown* case.

In November 1999, the nine African Americans who integrated Central High School received the Congressional Gold Medal. The medal is the highest civilian award in the United States. Those who received the medal were Minnijean Brown, Elizabeth Echford, Ernest Green, Thelma Mothershed, Melba Patillo Beals, Gloria Ray, Terrence Roberts, Jefferson Thomas, and Carlotta Walls.

WEB SITES
WWW.ABDOPUB.COM

Would you like to learn more about *Brown v. Board of Education*? Please visit **www.abdopub.com** to find up-to-date Web site links about *Brown v. Board of Education* and other American moments. These links are routinely monitored and updated to provide the most current information available.

An African-American man uses a segregated entrance to a movie theater in Belzoni, Mississippi.

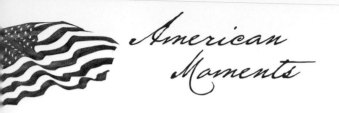

GLOSSARY

chancellor: a judge in a court of chancery.

civil rights: the individual rights of a citizen, such as the right to vote or freedom of speech.

Court of Chancery: a court in Delaware that handles disputes in which no one has broken a law. The court of chancery also deals with cases involving corporations.

dean: a person at a university who is in charge of guiding students.

detrimental: harmful.

discrimination: treating a group of people unfairly based on characteristics such as race, class, or gender.

doctrine: a legal principle that has been set down by precedent, or previous rulings.

eradicate: to do away with something.

inherent: a natural quality in a person, thing, or situation.

integration: ending segregation. To desegregate, specifically in schools or other public places that were segregated.

46

lawsuit: a case brought to court because of a perceived wrong.

manifesto: a declaration of views or intentions.

opinion: a legal explanation of a judge's decision on a particular case.

Radical Republicans: members of the Republican Party who were
    committed to freeing the slaves before the Civil War (1861–1865).
    After the war, Radical Republicans fought for equality for freed slaves.

segregation: to put social or political barriers around certain groups of
    people based on characteristics such as race, class, or gender.

switchyard: a place where trains are assembled and railroad cars are
    switched.

tangible: able to be perceived, especially by touch.

unconstitutional: not consistent with the Constitution.

vagrancy: wandering around without employment or a home. Vagrancy is
    often considered a crime.